Releasing Sorrow Embracing Joy
A Journey Through Life
By: Kathryn Anderson Sirven
© 2019

"Honor and majesty surround him; strength and joy fill his dwelling." **1 Chronicles 16:27**

"And Nehemiah continued, 'Go and celebrate with a feast of rich foods and sweet drinks, and share gifts of food with people who have nothing prepared. This is a sacred day before our Lord. Don't be dejected and sad, for the joy of the Lord is your strength!'...So the people went away to eat and drink at a festive meal, to share gifts of food, and to celebrate with great joy because they had heard God's words and understood them." **Nehemiah 8:10, 12**

*"You keep track of all my sorrows,
You have collected all my tears in your bottle.
You have recorded each one in your book."* **Psalm 56:8**

*"Those who have been ransomed by the Lord will return.
They will enter Jerusalem singing,
crowned with everlasting joy.
Sorrow and mourning will disappear,
and they will be filled with joy and gladness."* **Isaiah 51:11**

"He will wipe every tear from their eyes, and there will be no more death or sorrow or crying or pain. All these things are gone forever." **Revelation 21:4**

Every person experiences periods of sorrow and joy in their life. Sometimes these periods are intertwined and sometimes they are distinct. The following collection of poetry reflects every aspect of my life. There were times of great loss and times of great gain, but God has been there through everything and for that, I am truly grateful. The poems in this collection are in no particular order to show the journey through life that every person goes through. There are ups and downs in every life. These poems show that even in the low points of life, God is always there.

This collection is dedicated to the following people:
To Christ, my Savior, who, without His strength, this collection would not have been written.
To Megan who has never let me down.
To my friends at Louisiana College who loved me and nurtured me while I was there.
To my friends at the UL at Lafayette BCM who have helped me grow as a Christian.
To my parents who made me the person that I have become.
To Brandonn, my heart is always yours. Thank you for teaching me to love again.
To my pastors, Bro. Steve and Bro. Perry. Thank you for teaching me about the God I serve.
To all of you who, through the years, have encouraged my writing.
To everyone else who has touched my life through these years.

May God bless each one of you.

This book has been published in memory of Dr. Perry Sanders, former pastor of First Baptist Church Lafayette, LA

Alone

I could tell by the look
In my father's eyes
That the things he was saying
Were not a bunch of lies.

I knew deep inside
The fact that my father was gone
I could not hide.
And now I'm left alone.

Heartbroken

He stood there holding a dozen roses
With broken stems
The rain poured and the storms came
As he walked out into the cold

His heart's been broken
His life's changed
The love of his life has now become
The one who hurt him

He reaches out a hand
In the cold dark night
Searching for a friend

Someone to calm his fears
Someone to heal
The shattered pieces of his soul
Someone to heal
His wounded heart and make him whole

Deteriorating

Built upon the Rock
This nation once stood tall
And now that the foundation is failing,
This nation will crumble and fall

I stand and look around
As this nation falls apart.
From the morals it once had,
America now departs.

A Perfect World

Lost in a world
All of her own
A little girl sits
As a queen on her throne

She lives in a world
Where violence doesn't exist
Where no one locks a door
Or puts up a fence

Guns do not exist
In this world without fear
It's a world of love
And a world of cheer.

Broken

I come before You broken
Fallen on my knees
Every scar has been reopened
Every wound begins to bleed

Weary from the journey,
I seek Your holy face
I long to feel Your love
And for Your arms' embrace.

Anyway

So many times I've failed
And walked the other way
But He loves me anyway

So many times I've tried
To live my life MY way
And He still loves me anyway

Despite my lies,
My sin and my shame,
Jesus Christ loves me ANYWAY!

Dear Mommy
(Letter from the Womb)

I'm alive, you know.
I have hands; I have feet.
I'm alive, you see.
I have a heart that loudly beats.

I know you really can't hear me,
But I have something I must share:
I want to live and love and grow
I want to breathe fresh air.

I know it's okay and legal and all,
But Mommy, I'm begging, please:
Let me live life to the fullest
So that when I die, I'll die in peace.

I want to die knowing
I've lived life to the full
I want to die knowing
My life was not dull.

My Prayer

You smiled when I was happy.
Your heart broke when I was sad.
You were patient when mistakes were made.
You calmed me when I got mad.

My soul longs to feel that peace.
My heart longs to know You're there.
I want to know if You're still listening.
I need to know if You still care.

Helpless and Hopeless

Spiraling downward
In a helpless heap
Trying desperately
This depression to beat

I look all around
And all I see
Is a wall of darkness
Black as can be

Where am I?
How did I get here?
Can someone please help me?
I'm lost and I'm scared.

Depressed

Sitting in a room
With a gun to my head
Wishing someone cared
Wishing I was dead

Out of my darkness
My hurt and despair
I find a friend
Who'll always be there

He listens to me and consoles me
And tells me it's okay
He comforts me and reassures me
That I can face another day

I Long

I long for the peace
That once flooded my soul
I long for the feeling
That once made me feel whole

I long for the knowing
I once had in my heart
I long to be saved
And not torn apart

Where has it gone—
This feeling of hope?
It's gone down the drain
Like an old bar of soap.

No More Pain
(Revelation 21:4)

Sitting at the window
Watching the falling rain
Hoping that the raindrops
Will wash away the pain

Confusion settles in
All hope is gone
Tears fall down
The pain still isn't gone

When will it end?
Only Jesus knows
The pain will end
When our faith in Him grows.

Revelation 21:4 (NLT) - He will wipe every tear from their eyes, and there will be no more death or sorrow or crying or pain. All these things are gone forever.

Like A Child

Like a child to her mother
In the middle of a storm,
So run I to You, Father
To keep me safe and warm

Like a child to his father
When a bully runs the show,
When Satan starts hounding,
To Your loving arms I go.

Like a child who has been wounded
Cries out for Mom and Pop
So my soul cries out to You, Lord
Wanting the pain to stop

Thank You, Friend

You walked into my life
When no one else was there
You held on to my hand
When no one seemed to care

You listened
With attentive ears
You never once
Belittled my fears

You never once tried
My problems to solve
You only always tried
My fears to resolve

You gave me hope
In the midst of my fear
You listened to me
And dried my tears

Thank you, friend,
For what you have done
Your friendship has pointed me
To God's Son

Live the Life

We walk day-by-day
Living in our own place
Do we see those around us hurting?
Do we see the pain on their face?

Jesus came to Earth
To heal those in pain
And all He asks of us
Is that we should do the same.

If we walk where Jesus walked
Endure the pain and strife,
We'll prove to those who are watching
That we can life the life

Prove to the world that we can share
Prove that we can love
Prove that Jesus wants them
To live with Him above.

Emptiness

There's an emptiness in my eyes–
A cry for something more
There's an emptiness in my soul–
As I find my life a bore

There's an emptiness in my mind–
A place for Satan to run
There's an emptiness in my life–
I feel I'm the only one

The only one to suffer
The things that I've been through
The only one to be afraid–
The only one confused

But then I hear a still, small voice
That brings me comfort and cheer
"Be still, My child, and rest in Me.
I've been there. I am near."

Life Goes On

When the wheels stop turning
And the fires stop burning
Life goes on

When the baby stops crying
And people stop prying
Life goes on

When the world stops spinning
And Christ starts winning
Life goes on

Life goes on despite the pain
And it goes on despite the rain
Life goes on

Life goes on beyond the grave
Life goes on beyond your days
Life goes on

I Said, "Yes"

With the Savior facing the cross
Looking into the face of loss
Peter said, "no".

With His word on the table
Feeling I'm not able
I said, "no".

With a gun to her head,
Looking at the face of death,
Cassie said, "yes".

In the face of hardship,
Of grief and of pain,
I said, "yes".

Yes to God's leadership;
Yes to His hands;
Yes to His calling
To go where He sends.

Who is He to Me?

Some say He's a prophet
Some say He's a king
Some say He's the healer
Of all of their disease.

Some say He works miracles;
Some say He raises the dead;
Some say He makes the water to wine
And the stones to wholesome bread.

I say He's my Savior;
I say He's my King;
I say He's the Lord
Over everything.

God's Love

Why would God love me?
I've failed so many times
He loves me despite my cheating–
He loves me despite my lies

Why would God love me?
Why would He send His Son?
Why would God love me?
Why would He die for this sinful one?

His love is unexplainable
It's love beyond degree
It takes an unconditional love
To love someone like me

At the Foot of the Cross

Ashamed, I look up
With the hammer in my hand
Wounded, I look up
In search of Your guiding hand

At the foot of the cross
Within my hand, a nail,
I turn to the cross
And turn away from Hell.

I kneel at the cross
With nothing more to give
Facing my Savior's death
For by His grace, I live

Hammer and nail in hand,
I see His blood falling down.
At the foot of my Savior,
My life I now lay down.

Visions of Hell

You stand at the gates
Awaiting the call of your name
For some it means victory
For others it means Lakes of Flames

You hear your name
Yes, it's true
God called your name
He's waiting for you

As you walk to the gates,
You think of all the "good things" done
But when it comes to Jesus
Your score sits at none

You say you've been a good kid
You played all the right games
God says it's not good enough
And you are sent into the Lake of Flames

My Prayer

You smiled when I was happy.
Your heart broke when I was sad.
You were patient when mistakes were made.
You calmed me when I got mad.

My soul longs to feel that peace.
My heart longs to know You're there.
I want to know if You're still listening.
I need to know if You still care.

Reach Out

You see them on the corner
You see them on the street
You never know if they are Christians
So reach out to those you meet

You may not have tomorrow
Or even the rest of today
So reach out to those you meet
And show them Jesus is the Way

You may see them in the mall
You may see them at school
They are the ones labeled "good kids"
Who always follow the rules

You may not even recognize them
It could be your closest friend
If you don't reach out to them
You may regret it in the end

Our Message

Whether one, or all,
Whether short, or tall,
Whether young, or old,
Whether shy, or bold,

From the depths of the sea,
To the furthermost star,
We must make known
Whose we are

We stand for the One
Who created the earth
We stand for the One
Who gave us new birth
We must proclaim the name of Jesus

Decisions, Decisions, Decisions

Struggling with the will to live
Wondering how I would survive
My struggles seemed endless – all hope was gone.
But somehow I made it--I made it alive.

I chose to live
In case you didn't know.
My life has gotten better
Now that the reasons for sadness I know.

Everywhere

In the sunset, I see His peacefulness.
In the warmth, I feel His love.
In the stars, I see His handiwork
That flows from His home above.

In the storms, I feel His anger
At something on the Earth
In the fluffy clouds, I see His hand
Which has protected me from my birth.

Friends

Friends were made for sharing
All the good times and the bad.
Friends were made for telling
About the fun you had.

Friends were made for keeping
Throughout all the years.
Friends were made for caring
Even when you're in tears.

Friends were made for telling
About the good times and bad
In times of happiness and sadness
And joy and tears.

A Cry Out To God

Wash me, Lord
Make me clean
Put within me
Your Spirit to be seen

Help me, Lord
To be a vessel for You
Let Your light shine
In all that I do

Heal me, Lord
From the wounds that pierce deep
Teach me, Lord
To lay my burdens at Your feet

I cry out within me
From depths I know not
For You, Lord, to meet me
At this very spot.

Take me and teach me
And show me the way
Hold me close to You
So I won't fall astray

Strength to Stand

As we walk
Hand in hand
Jesus gives me
The strength to stand

Through the darkness
And when life is grand
Jesus gives me
The strength to stand

To stand for what is right
Even when I'm not sure
To stand up and fight
Even when I'm insecure

Thank You, Jesus,
For the strength to stand
Thank You, Jesus,
For walking with me hand-in-hand.

Victory

So you didn't win the gold,
Or the silver, or the bronze,
Maybe you came in fourth,
Or maybe you just froze

You couldn't remember your routine
You were as nervous as a cat
At least you made it through
You didn't falter on the mat

The Christian life is similar
To this great competition or game
There's more to win for Jesus
The gold is not the same

For the world, the victory is a medal;
For Christ, the conquest is a soul.
You may not reach your all-time best
But at least you reached the goal

Wandering

A wandering soul reaches out
To find a helping hand
A quivering soul steps out
Upon the shifting sand

A longing soul reaches out
To find someone who cares
A hurting soul reaches out
To find someone there

Is there a heart out there
Who will reach out to just one?
Is there a hand out there
Who will help a single person?

I will be the one
To share Christ's love
I will be the one
Living for the Father above.

Restore Me

The voices – they play
Over in my head
Telling me lies –
I'm better off dead

If I had the power,
Trust me, I would –
I'd turn them off
Like I know I should

God, You have the power
By the blood of the cross
To restore my sanity
And all that I've lost

God, You have the power
To heal my mind
To restore my thoughts
To Your sacrifice

A Christmas Gift

Looking into the face of a baby
She really had no clue
What the Infant in her arms
Would grow up to do

She knew the Child was special—
She knew He was divine
She did not know that He'd grow up
To change the water into wine

She knew she was holding royalty
She knew it was the face of a King
But she did not know that her baby
Would be no earthly King

She did not know God's ultimate plan
She only knew her part
From this Infant Child within her arms
God's redemption plan would start

She did not know the pain she'd face
When Christ was nailed to a tree
But she did know the truth
That He died for you and me.

Luke 2:19 - "But Mary kept all these things in her heart and thought about them often."

Memories

I know very soon
I'll have to say, "good-bye"
It'll be rough
And I know we'll cry

I know we'll be forever
And I know it's hard to see
How we'll be together
Friend, you are my memory

Wishes

Wishes are like rivers
Always changing as they go
Some are never granted
Some people change them as they grow

Wishes are like precious crystal
Preserved through the years
When wishes are shattered
Like a river flow the tears

Lines

Looking in from the outside
I see exclusiveness of the groups
Their closed meetings
In tight circles

I see the destruction of the groups
That only God can stop
I see the tightness of the group
That no one can loosen

From the inside they don't see
The pain and hardships they cause
Their eyes are blind
To the lines they have drawn

I see the inflexibility of the lines
I dare not cross
I see the reality of the pain
That outsiders feel

The line of religion
The line of race
The line of creed
The line of age

Destructive lines
That Satan forms
That keeps a group
Forever torn

My Prayer

Here I sit waiting
Waiting on You, Father
Waiting for You to work.

Why are you waiting?
Stand, My child.
Walk, My child.
Listen, My child.

Father, forgive me
I am standing.
Why am I standing?
For me, My child

Father, forgive me
I am walking.
Where am I going?
With me, My child

Father, forgive me
I am listening.
What are You saying?
Be still, My child,
And know that I am God.

Inner Beauty

Beyond the swimsuit
There's nothing to hide.
Beauty doesn't count.
It's what's on the inside.

Get rid of the makeup.
Get rid of the hair spray.
'Cause on the inside,
You're really okay.

Nobody's perfect
But no one should care
It shouldn't matter
If other people stare.

Jesus Loves Me

He loves me in the brightest sunshine
He loves me in the gloomiest rain
He loves me through the happiest of times
He loves me through the deepest of my pain.

He is always there through the wonderful times,
Through the gayest happiness and the saddest tears,
He is always there through the horrible times
Through the highest joy and the deepest fears,

He is faithful until death and the end.
His smile is as broad as a road is wide.
He is forever your closest friend.
In Him you can continue to confide.

Jesus loves the children
Each and every one.
He even loves the adults
In spite of what they've done.

John 3:16 - "For God loved the world so much that he gave his one and only Son, so that
everyone who believes in him will not perish but have eternal life."

He's Always There

In the sunshine
And the rain,
Through the laughter
And the pain,
He's always there.

Through the happiness
And the tears,
Through the joy
And the fears,
He's always there.

He's faithful
To the end.
He's forever
Your best friend.
Jesus is always there.

They Came – I Come

To see a baby in a manger—they came
To hear a child with infinite wisdom—they came
To bow down and worship—to hear and to learn
They came to the Savior for Whom their hearts yearn
To hear a man teaching of mysterious things—they came
To see a miracle preformed before their eyes—they came
To bow down and worship—to hear and to learn
They came to the Savior for Whom their hearts yearn
To see a man crucified between two thieves—they came
To see a grave—guarded—empty within—they came
To bow down and worship—to hear and to learn
They came to the Savior for Whom their hearts yearn
Seeking unfailing love and redemption—I come
To know Him as King, to know Him as Lord—I come
I come to my Savior—come to my Lord.
I come to my Father and listen to His word.

To bow down and worship—to hear and to learn
I come to the Savior for Whom my heart yearns
With nothing left to give Him—I come
With nothing but empty hands—I come
I come to worship my King
I come to worship my Lord
Forever to His presence—I come
To His tender forgiveness—I come
To His love unending and His grace unknown—I come
To bow down and worship—to hear and to learn
I come to the Savior for Whom my heart yearns
I come to bow down and worship—to hear and to learn
I come to the Savior for Whom my heart yearns

Luke 2:15-17 - " When the angels had returned to heaven, the shepherds said to each other,
"Let's go to Bethlehem! Let's see this thing that has happened, which the Lord has told us
about." They hurried to the village and found Mary and Joseph. And there was the baby, lying in
the manger. After seeing him, the shepherds told everyone what had happened and what the
angel had said to them about this child."

Symphony

Life is a symphony
And God is the conductor.
The instruments are all the time
Being tuned

Life is a symphony
And I am an instrument
Playing--all the time
Being used

Life is a symphony
And God is the conductor
He leads me to play
The music as He writes

Life is a symphony
And I am an instrument
I learn to play
Beautiful music as the Master likes

Life is a symphony
Its music -- a soulful ballad
Its music -- a pop hit
God's music -- forever ringing

Life is a symphony
Its rhythm -- a slow dance
Its rhythm -- a jazz hit
God's music -- a forever offering

If Mary Had Said No

If Mary had said no,
Would God have still sent His Son?
If Mary had said no,
Would Jesus have come to save everyone?

If Mary had said no,
Would there be no hope for the world?
If Mary had said no,
Would there be more people out in the cold?

If Mary had said no,
Would the disciples have had Someone to follow?
If Mary had said no,
Would the Pharisees have Someone to put down?

If Mary had said no,
Would God's love have been demonstrated?
If Mary had said no,
Would Jesus' blood have been shed?

But Mary said yes,
And much to our delight,
Brought into this world
A brilliant and glorious Light

A Longing

I long for a world
Full of care.
I long for a world
That looks at something besides our hair.

I long for a world
That looks at your heart
I long for a world
In which beauty has no part.

I long for a world
Full of hope.
Not for a world
High on dope.

God's Always There

He's always there for me—He really cares
He's always there for me—when I am scared
He always greets me with a happy face
He always helps me win the race

He's always there with a caring smile
He always helps me go the extra mile
He loves beyond the point of grace
I can see it in His face
His smile is always there
To show me that He cares

He listens with attentive ears
He always tries to calm my fears
He sent His Son for the world to see
That He really loves and takes care of me

My Friend

I call you "my friend"
Because you care.
I call you "my friend"
Because you're always there.

I call you "my friend"
Because of your warm smile.
I call you "my friend"
Because you go with me the extra mile.

I call you "my friend"
Because in your arms
I can survive
All of life's storms.

To the End

Although the road I've traveled
In New Orleans
Is coming to an end
And I'll have to say good-bye,
I am reminded that we'll
Always be friends.

In tough times,
You stood beside me.
Through times,
You've been my friend.
We'll always be friends
Until the very end.

Nobody Knows

Alone in the world
Seems like nobody cares
Pain overwhelms you
Burdens are too much to bear.

Nobody hears your cries for help
Nobody sees your pain.
Nobody seems to realize
That life is not a game.

Nobody realizes there is another way.
Nobody notices your life is not great.
Nobody thinks you are hurting
Until it is too late.

I Live In A Nation

I live in a nation
Where violence has no end
I live in a nation
Where Death is a friend

I live in a nation
Where people do not care
They'll kill for a reason
As simple as the color of your hair

I live in a nation
Of which I want no part
I live in a nation
Of people without hearts

When will we realize
That this nation is ill?
When the prisons, institutes,
And graveyards we fill.

Wandering

A wandering soul reaches out
To find a helping hand
A quivering soul steps out
Upon the shifting sand.

A longing soul reaches out
To find someone who cares
A hurting soul reaches out
To find someone there.

Is there a heart out there
Who will reach just one?
Is there a hand out there
Who will help a single person?

I will be the one
To share Christ's love.
I will be the one
Living for the Father above.

Our Message

Whether one or all,
Whether short or tall,
We all have a message to proclaim.

Whether young or old,
Whether shy or bold,
We all have a name to proclaim.

From the depths of the sea,
To the farthest star,
We must make known
Who we are.

We stand for the One
Who created the earth.
We stand for the One
Who gives us new birth.

Where Are You?

"We'll always be forever,"
You said with a smile upon your face.
We'd always be together;
You'd help me win the race.

Well, where are you?
You said you'd love me always.
It was a love that wouldn't die.
But now that we're not together,

I'm a river that has run dry.
Well, where are you?
You said you'd never forget me
And with that thought, I left.

Now that we're in different cities,
And your memory is all I have,
Where in life are you?
Have you forgotten me?

Have you pushed me out of your mind?
Have you moved on with your life?
Am I just a memory?
Or are we friends for life?

Leprosy of the Heart

Uncaring – unfeeling
This leprosy of the heart
So callused and needy
This leprosy of the heart

Wanting to live – wishing to die
With leprosy of the heart
So desperate and lonely
With leprosy of the heart

In need of healing – in need of freedom
From leprosy of the heart
Only Jesus can save me
From leprosy of the heart

On Wings

I've fallen down and I can't get up
I'm worn out and tired and can't find rest
I hunger and thirst without satisfaction

I long to rise up and soar as an eagle
I long to run the race without getting tired
I long to find satisfaction in God alone
On His wings, I will soar

In His strength,
I will run
Under His shelter,
I will find fulfillment

Good-bye, Friend

I see the laughter;
I see the tears.
I see the brave;
I see their fears.

I see the love
That we lived by.
I see the pain
Behind saying "good-bye".

I see the faces of those
I'm leaving behind.
Their smiles are playing
Over in my mind.

I see the pain
That I went through.
I see those friends
That I could run to.

I see the potential
In eyes younger than mine.
I see them as men and women
Who will make the future bright.

It is to those faces
That I want to say a word:
Stay strong, stay faithful,
And stay close to the Lord.

To a Friend

Misunderstandings of words and actions
Are what tore the two of us apart
Now, as I try to understand
I don't know how to start.

I had been hurt
Beyond what I could bear
And I listened to you half-heartedly
Just like I didn't care.

I want you to know
That I want to start over again
All has been forgiven now.
Will you still be my friend?

I wanted so much
To make it all go away
That I forgot about our friendship
I forgot about today.

Through all the pain and hardship—
Forever to the end—
I want you to know that always
I want to be your friend.

The Answer

Alone in the darkness
Looking at the bunk above
I think about God's mercy
I think about His love

I think about the calmness—
The serenity of the bay
Then I think about the cross
And I think about His grave.

I cry out into the darkness
Searching for an answer.

Then the very next morning
With the sun shining brightly
I see a cross on the beach
On the other side of the bay

That is the answer
That I have been searching for.
Thank You, Jesus, for the cross
Thank You, Jesus, for the answer.

Fitting the Mold

What will happen when we grow up?
Will we know what to do?
Will we be conforming to the mold
That our parents had to?

Will we dare to be different—
Dare to break the mold?
Or will we live our lives content
To fit in within the fold.

"What would Jesus do?"
Is the question of the time.
Will our generation stand out,
Or to this world be confined?

Oceans

The waves rush over me uncontrollably
I feel so many things to try to explain
I feel an undying love
I feel an emotional attachment
That I have never felt before
I feel something that I can't really describe

A woman's heart is but an ocean
And you have begun to swim in it.
You may get lost in this vast deep ocean.
You may drown in this wonderful, tender ocean

I will forever love you
No matter what happens
You will always be able to swim
In my ocean of my emotions.

In Memory of a Loved One

When you left the earth,
You left a lot behind
You left a hole in my heart
And a void in my mind

You left behind a memory
That's sometimes hard to bear
As I sit here wishing
That you were still there

The hole in my heart
Will heal one day
When in Heaven with you
And Jesus I'll stay.

(Written in memory of my Memaw)

He's Always There For Me

He's always there for me
He really cares.
He's always there for me
When I am scared.
He always greets me
With a happy face.
He always helps me
Win the race.

He's always there
With a smile.
He always helps me
Go the extra mile.
He loves beyond
The point of grace
I can see it
In His face.

His smile is
Always there
To show me
That He cares
He listens
With attentive ears.
He always tries
To calm my fears.

He sent His Son
For the world to see
That He really takes care of
And loves me.

Surrender

Why is it so hard, God,
To look only to You
When You see only me?

Why is it so hard, Jesus,
To give my life to You
When You gave Your life for me?

Why is it so hard, Father,
To love only You
When Your heart breaks constantly for me?

Why is it so hard, Lord,
To live inside Your love
When it forever shines on me?

Dying to myself
And living for You—
Why, my God,
Is it so hard to do?

I wake up every day
To my old habits and desires.
Re-light within my soul
Your never-ending fire.

Hugs Forever

They met for the first time
And their arms ached for embrace
He reaches out to touch her
A smile creeps across her face

Could this be the one God has
For a weary soul?
Could this be the person God made
To make her life whole?

They embrace for what seems like forever
Until the sun begins to set—-
Until the day begins to end--
Forever that day they met.

Anew

Lord, give me a passion to see
What You would have for me

Lord, rekindle the fire
And renew my desire

Lord, give me a passion for the lost
To reach them no matter the cost

Lord, help me to obey
And walk in Your ways

Lord, consume me with Your grace
As I seek Your holy face

Empty Hands

I have nothing left to give
Except for my empty hands
Fill them up, Father,
With riches from Your lands

Use my hands for Your work
Help me keep them clean
Help me use them for Your glory
And use them for my King

Give me a reason to celebrate
Give me a reason to sing
Take these empty hands of mine
As an humble offering

Use these hands to work miracles
In bodies, minds, and souls
Use these hands for Your Kingdom
To reach Your Heavenly goals

Take this simple offering
And use it in Your name
To change the lives of people
So they'll never be the same

Use my hands to reach out
To all those lost in sin
Help me reach out to lost sheep
And them into Your folds bring in

Beyond the Mask

I see you here
I see you there
I see beyond
The mask you wear

I see your wounds
I see your shame
I feel your hurt
I feel your pain

Beyond the mask
I see your face
I see a human
Saved by Divine grace

There's nothing to hide
Let me show you
Of the glorious grace
When His love shines through

Abused For Me

The nails pierced His skin
The thorns pierced His brow
The whip tore His skin
He took the physical abuse for me

The crowd cried, "Crucify!"
Pilate washed his hands
The soldiers mocked His name
He took the verbal abuse for me

The stares, the jeers
The laughing, the mocking
The loneliness, the pain
He took the abuse for me

Rainbows and Promises

A rainbow graces the sky
After a springtime rain
God's rainbow graces my heart
After a time of pain

A rainbow brightens the clouds
After the summer storm
A rainbow mends the pieces
Of a heart once torn

A rainbow graced the sky
After a blazing fire
God's rainbow is a promise
To fulfill His own desires

God's covenant is a rainbow—
A promise yet to come—
A sign from a Holy Father
That He'll never leave you alone.

Written after the First Baptist Church Lafayette burned down in June of 1999

No More Band-Aids in Heaven

No bumps or bruises
No cuts or sprains
No more Band-Aids in Heaven

No need for Neosporin
No need for Cortisone
No more Band-Aids in Heaven

No bees that sting
No dogs that bite
No more Band-Aids in Heaven

No more disease
No more death
No more Band-Aids in Heaven

No broken bones
No broken hearts
No more Band-Aids in Heaven

No divorced families
No broken homes
No more Band-Aids in Heaven

No more pain
No more grief
No more Band-Aids in Heaven

Running

Far from His plan
I run away
Away from His voice
I run away
Into the darkness
I run away
To hide myself from Him
I run away
Into the forest of darkness and sin
I run away
To the underbrush of secrecy
I run away

Verbal Stones

Words that sting fly through the air
Words of hurt, of anger, and despair
Words that leave wounds open to bleed
Words of hatred because of race or creed

Verbal stones fly without much care
Leaving the recipient deep in despair
Stones of anger and stones of rage
Leave you locked up like an animal in a cage

Words of compassion should these stones replace
Verbal stones should these kind words erase
Christ's words as our model
Verbal stones we will dispel

Calming Savior

Terror fills her face
As he comes into the room
Rage fills his eyes
And she endures the agony again

He slaps her and kicks her
He tells her she's no good
He leaves her there bleeding
And shaking in her skin

He tells her she can't say a word
The secret's deep inside
It eats away at her insides
It steals her innocence away

She cries out in agony
But no one sees her tears
Buried deep inside of her
Is pain no one can heal

But one day she finds a Savior
A Friend who calms her soul
A Father above all fathers
Who longs to make her whole

Dark Songs

Almighty, Omnipotent Lord,
Show Thyself again.
I need Thy healing and Thy touch
I need Thine outstretched hand.

Thou wilt keep in perfect peace
The mind steadfast on Thee.
Thou wilt comfort the wounded heart
And attend to the bended knee.

Father, Savior, God and King,
Healer of my soul,
I need Thy calming, steadfast hand
To touch me and make me whole.

Free me from the dark within.
Shine Thy light on my heart.
Almighty Jesus, Father of light,
Come and do Thy part.

Heal my heart, and my mind.
Make my spirit free.
Come and live inside my soul
And make the darkness flee.

Only You

Help me, Lord,
In worshiping
To see only You

Help me, Lord,
In singing
To sing to only You

Help me, Lord,
When I'm falling
To look to only You

Help me, Lord
In my daily life
To live for only You

Faithful Legacy

'Well done, My faithful servant,"
He heard his Savior say
As he slipped away from this world
That fateful April day.

Though the world outside is laughing
Inside the walls, there's crying.
The flowers in the room – living –
Around the man who is dying.

He went to meet his Savior
He'd known for all his life
And left behind a legacy
For his family, friends, and wife.

He left a legacy of love and faith
For all he came across
The world he left behind that day
Will always feel the loss

A man of his word
To all that he met –
He was a friend and a role model
That none will forget.

Written in memory of my Dado

Revival

Hot coals rain down
Cleansing, healing
Helping, reviving
God, send Your coals

Raining on us
To cleanse us, to heal us
To help us to revive us
Send Your rain, Lord,

So that we may display
Your glory, Your renown
Your praise, Your power
Wash us clean, God,

Make us wholly Yours
Revive us, give us fire
Give us passion
Send Your revival on us

Unlovely Me

Broken and battered
Tossed by the storm
I come

Afraid and alone
Not a friend in the world
I come

You loved me—You died for me
You saved me
Unlovely as I am

Because You loved
The unlovely—the unworthy
Because You loved me

Everlasting Hope

Darkness falls
The way is lost
A cry for help resounds

Closing in
Around me now
The walls by which I'm bound

Light breaks through
Walls fall down
Christ's love abides to all

God sent His Son
As love personified
To redeem mankind from the fall

Looking up
To my only hope
He resides on Heaven's throne

He lived and died
On Calvary's tree
For a world He called His own

God Is

I can't give you what you need,
But God does
I can't answer all of your questions,
But God will

I can't always be there for you,
But God is
I won't always know what to say,
But God will

I can't love you unconditionally,
But God does
I can't die to save your life,
But God did

God will provide for you
He'll answer your questions
He'll be there for you
And love you unconditionally

The Heart of Worship

My broken and dirty toy–
I bring to my daddy to fix.
My scarred and tired spirit–
I bring to my Daddy to fix.

I trust my earthly father
To make it all better
How much more, God,
Will You make me whole?

With total trust
With complete surrender
With absolute assurance
I go to my Father

With tenderness
With awesome love
With perfect precision
He lifts me up

When I come to my daddy,
He fixes my toy.
When I come to my Daddy,
He heals my life.

I have no choice
But to worship Him
I have no choice
But to serve with my life

There Must Be More

I know He's my Savior
I know He's my Lord
But there must be more

I know He died
And rose again
But there must be more

There must be more to life
Than walking down the road
There must be more

I read my Bible
I pray daily
But there must be more

I see the pain around me
I see people hurting
Lord, there must be more

Beyond the cross
Beyond the grave
Lord, there must be more

The cross–the grave–
A risen Lord–
There's more to life than what is seen

Crossbeams

On a hill far away
Stands three sets of crossbeams
Between two thieves
Hangs a sinless man

Innocence surrounded by guilt
Humility surrounded by pride
Infinite love surrounded by hatred
Life surrounded by death

Blood flows from three crossbeams
Only one river can heal
From a sinful man, a request is made
A sinless Savior grants

Heaven beats Hell
Life beats death
Innocence beats guilt
On the crossbeams, Jesus wins

Casting Lots

At the foot of the cross
The soldiers cast lots
Completely unaware
Of the Savior's blood

At the foot of the cross
A cloak goes for a shekel
A heart goes for pride
The blood means nothing

At the foot of the cross
We stand casting lots
We try to work our way into Heaven
We ignore the blood pooling beside us

At the foot of the cross
The lot is cast
Christ has paid the price
And bought us

Isaiah 6:8

Lord I stand before You today
Afraid and unsure
Father, I hear Your call
So loud and clear

Lord I stand before You today
Prideful and unclean
Father, I am unworthy
To be touched by You

Lord I stand before You today
Broken and humble
Father, I am willing
To be used by You

At home or away,
In comfort and trial,
Here I am, Lord,
Send me

Isaiah 6:8 - Then I heard the Lord asking, "Whom should I send as a messenger to this people? Who will go for us?" I said, "Here I am. Send me."

Find Me Faithful

When I wake up in the morning,
And start every day the same
May those who walk behind me
Find me faithful

When I walk around on campus
Moving from class to class
May those who come behind me
Find me faithful

When I leave for home each afternoon
Worn out from a long, hard day
May those who come behind me
Find me faithful

When I lay my head on my pillow
I pray before I sleep
That those who came behind me
Found me faithful

When I complete my life
And I am long gone
May those who come behind me
Find me faithful

Wasted Time

A minute here
A minute there
A lot of wasted time
A lot of unused minutes

Wasted minutes
Wasted hours
Wasted days
A lot of unused time

Hours spent
Doing nothing
Should have been used
For God's work

Opportunities missed
Things undone
All lay dormant
In wasted time

Humble Worship

I bow before my Lord–
humbled–amazed–
That He would die for me–
sinful–broken.

I stand before my God–
in worship–in praise–
Of His love and grace–
unconditional–unending.

On my face before the cross–
I see His glory–
I see His grace–
The crimson flows—healing–forgiving.

One Day

Better is one day in Your courts
Singing Your praises
Listening to Your voice
Better is one day in Your house
Worshiping in spirit
Praying in earnest
Better is one day in Your courts
Interceding for saints
Praying for sinners
Than a thousand elsewhere
In Your presence, Lord,
Is where I want to be.

Oblivious

Help me, Lord,
In worship to You
To see only You

Help me, Lord,
In singing to You
To realize my audience is You

Help me, Lord,
In walking with You
To look up when I fall

Help me, Lord,
In my daily life
To live in a state of oblivion with You

Oblivious to my pain
Oblivious to my hurt
'Cause You, oh Lord, are my Savior

Desperate

A hungry infant cries out
Desperate for nourishment
An abandoned child longs
Desperate for that warm embrace

A thirsty deer searches
Desperate for water
A lonely soul reaches out
Desperate for companionship

Jesus Christ lived
Desperate for people
My Lord and Savior died
Desperate for souls

Hunger and Desperation

The baby crying for milk–
The toddler asking for juice–
Desperate for something to drink

The child hungry for lunch–
The teen searching for dinner–
Desperate for something to eat

The empty college student–
The hurting adult–
Desperate for healing and fulfillment

The loving God–
The sinless Savior–
Desperate to save

God – in desperation –
Ran to me – died for me
I – in hunger and desperation –
Cry out for Him to fill me.

Growing

Tiny hands and tiny feet
Tiny lungs and a heart that beats
Tiny eyes that dance and smile
Tiny love that lasts a while

Growing feet that run and play
Growing minds to learn the way
Growing hearts that learn to love
Growing understanding of God above

Childlike cries from bed at night
Childlike faith to calm the fright
Childlike wishes from a childlike heart
Childlike dreams started from a spark

Day-by-day and step-by-step
Little by little, with a little help
Tiny feet grow, run, and play
Tiny hearts learn, love, and pray

Written in honor of Rachel Claire Buckels born June 22, 2001

His Body – My Cross

The pain I've caused—
The lies I've told–
The life I've lived–
Beams on the cross

The anger I hide–
The bitterness inside–
The rage eating in me–
Nails in His body

His blood flows down
Covering the beams
His blood flows down
Covering the nails

Unholiness meets holiness
Unforgiveness meets forgiveness
Bitterness meets love eternal
On my cross on which He died

Before His Table

I come before Your table, Lord
Asking for Your amazing grace
To set me in Your presence, Lord
So I can feel You in this place

I know I've been unfaithful
I know I don't deserve it all
But You love me unconditionally.
And I'm grateful for Your call

It's in Your presence I find mercy
And in Your presence I find peace
It's in the glorious words You've spoken
That my soul finds great release

Forgive me, Father, for I have failed
I know I've made mistakes.
Your grace is all sufficient, Lord
To bring me to this place

Where I can worship freely
Come and bow before Your throne
Knowing my life is unworthy Lord
Knowing my strength is in You alone

My Gracious Lord and Savior,
My Redeemer and my King
Thank You for the cross You died on
Thank You for forgiving me

Holy Ground

Broken and humble
To His presence I come
Battered and worn
To His presence I come

The road beneath is rocky
The journey is so long
My battered soul I bring
And to His presence I come

The ground beneath my feet
Turns into solid ground
"My child," I hear His voice,
"Just listen. Turn around.

Release to Me your burden
Let My love surround
For the ground on which you are standing
In My presence is Holy Ground."

So to His arms I run
No matter who is around
For peace and love and comfort
I fall on Holy Ground.

I'm Sorry

I've hurt you more than I wanted to
I've blamed you for more than your share
I've made you angry for the way I've acted
I've made you wonder if I still care

I don't understand completely
What you're going through right now
But I'm trying hard to love you
Even though you make me mad

And I'm trying hard to understand
Forgive me for my insecurities
Forgive me for my ignorance
Help me to understand

I don't want you to be angry
I don't want you to be upset
But sometimes I don't know how to express myself
I'm very prone to anger

I'm prone to raising my voice
Please help me learn to control myself
Help me to stay out of trouble
Help me to keep the peace

Help me find a safe place
Help me learn to release my aggression
Help me learn to rely on God
As I try to make this marriage work

Christmas Memories

Gathered 'round the fire
Singing Christmas songs
With Mom at the piano
Oh has it been so long?

Silent nights and little towns
Jingle Bells and Deck the Halls
The First Noel and Three Wise Men
The words - I know them all

And as each Christmas draweth close
Those age-old songs I hear
Reminding me all the time
That at Christmas you aren't here

The tears - they overwhelm me
I cannot make them end
'Cause when you died
I lost in you a very special friend

Written in honor of and memory of my Dado Christmas 2006

The Man In The Back

It was Resurrection Sunday
As they all filed into church
A Man sat on the back row
And in the commotion didn't say a word
The organist started the prelude
As people slowly found their seats
Never realizing on the back row
Was Someone they needed to meet
The music was very moving
The sermon wasn't shallow
But no one in that sanctuary
Was prepared for what would follow
Many decisions were made that day
But before the postlude could start
The Man on the back row slowly stood.
"Pastor, I have something on my heart."
The pastor said, "Alright.
Come and speak Your heart."
And as the Man walked to the front
More apparent became His scars
The congregation settled back down
And no one rose to leave
Not a sound was heard in that sanctuary
Not a cough or even a sneeze
"I am the One of Whom you sing.
I am the crucified Lord.
I stand before you and proclaim
I am risen forever more."
The congregation said not a word
As Jesus took His seat
There was blood and dirt on the carpet
Coming from His barren feet
The pastor slowly stood
And began to sing a hymn
"God sent His Son, they called Him Jesus…"
And the congregation joined right in.
Because He lives, I know for a fact
Tomorrow we can face
The congregation left that morning
Their lives forever changed.

Pain and Forgiveness

Rage wells up inside
From a source I cannot know
Anger overflows
And casts me in its shadow
The pain I feel from scars I have
Is almost too much to bear
To run from the pain would be pointless
It seems to be everywhere
My life has been changed
By one lousy course of events
And the hefty price of fear
I have paid ever since
No one can know my anger
None can know my pain
None can know the fear I have
That it will happen all over again
From the anger, pain and fear
No one can bring relief
Until the deed is punished
And there is an end to my grief
My heart has been broken
My spirit has been jarred
My hope in man is vanished
My mind is forever scarred
The pain you caused in my life
I will never forget
The action I never took
I will always regret
My only precious hope right now
Is in a God I can only hear
I need His peace and presence
To sweep away this fear
The cross of Christ stands tall
On an old abandoned hill
Upon that hideous tree
Christ died to pay the bill
"My grace is sufficient for you,"
I hear my Savior say
For it is only by His grace
That I make it through the day

By His gracious hand
I will make it through
And only by His grace

Will I be able to forgive you
The grace of God abounds
Where sin abides the most
But between the two of us
I need His grace the most
I need His grace to make it through
I need His grace to live
I need His grace to stand before you
And say to you, "I forgive."
I forgive you for the pain you've caused
For the shame and anger, too
I forgive you by the grace of God
Because He has forgiven me, too.

Within the Blood

Humbled at the cross I kneel
Astounded by Your grace
Basking in the crimson flood
Looking into Your face

Compassion mixed with grace I see
With forgiveness and Your love
Mercy for my every need
With power from above

The hope of all mankind
Hung on a Roman tree
And from Your side, blood runs down
Healing - cleansing me

Freeing me from anger and pain
Freeing me from loss
Freeing me from grief and shame
At the foot of the old rugged cross

Forgiven and free I stand
In the healing flood
Knowing that my only hope
Is found within the blood

Lord, help me now with open arms
To forgive those who wronged me
To share with them the love of Christ
And secure their eternity.

My Testimony

Bloodied and broken
Down life's road I came
Entangled in my past
Searching for freedom
From despair and shame
Wanting relief that lasts

Bloodied and broken
On life's road I meet
A Man who knows my past
Giving out freedom
For those in need
Sharing my pain at last

Cautious and curious
This Man - I greet
And ask Him for His name
Softly and gently
This Man - He speaks
"I am Healer of all pain"

"Forgiven and healed,
You will walk
Forever and always."
Revived and joyful,
With all I'll talk
Of the day that I was saved.

Quiet Release

The clouds roll in.
The sky turns black.
The rain falls down.
Will it ever slack?
The pain is real.
The hurt is deep.
Into a darkened soul
Revenge begins to creep

Darkness all around.
No end can be seen.
Hate creeps into my soul
For the treatment I received.
Fear creeps in and
My heart grows hard.
Unknown to the world,
My soul falls dark

I've lost my hope in humanity.
I've lost my hope in God.
I've lost my hope in relief from pain
Whilst I treads upon this sod.
I wonder if my soul will survive
Despite the raging pain.
I wonders if I'll love anew
Despite from whence I came.

I hear within a quiet voice
That tells me I am loved.
It resounds in the walls of my soul
From the Father in Heaven above.
The pain in my heart subsides
The aching begins to cease.
From my hurt and anger
In God I find release.
My hard heart melts within me
The need for revenge is relieved
For in me Lord and Savior,
I've found everything I need

Blessed Peace

Troubled and weary
I bow before the throne
Confused and unsure
I feel so alone

Searching for answers
I fall on my face
The only answer I find
Is in this Holy Place

Grace for the moment
Wisdom for the day
Peace for the hour
In His presence I will stay

A blessed peace I find
While bowing at His feet
This blessed peace I'll share
With all those I will meet.

Jehovah Jireh

Upon this mountaintop I stand
Waiting on a word from the Lord
Not knowing which way I'm going
Not knowing who to trust

I have so many needs
That I cannot fulfill
Searching for answers to questions
That crowd the corners of my mind

Jehovah Jireh meets me there
Upon the mountainside
"I will answer your every question
And for every need provide.

The questions that you have
Are common to the world
So all I ask of you, My child
Is to trust My every word

Trust me when I say okay
Trust me when you're afraid
Trust me when you've walked away
From My tender care."

Jehovah Jireh cares for me
He fills my every need
Jehovah Jireh fills my soul
With a blessed peace

Justified

Enraptured and captured
By Your love divine
To hear Your gentle voice,
"Blessed child, you are Mine."

Embraced and surrounded
By Your grace so rich and full
To hear Your voice with mercy,
"Your sins I have annulled."

Enlivened and aflame
With a fire deep within
To hear Your voice call to me,
"Blessed child, you are free from sin."

Enlightened and empowered
By Your power, I stand
To share Your love and grace
With every living man.

My Giant Slayer

Giants all around me
The world is closing in
Options I've run out of
So I must search within
The strength I need to fight
On earth I cannot find
There is no place in this world
From these giants I can hide
The giant called "Fear of Failure"
The one called "Not Good Enough"
The giant called "Fear of Change"
This giant bunch is rough

So to my knees I go
For that's where war begins
The battle becomes sacred
For Jesus Christ steps in
"To the giant called 'Fear of Failure,'
In Me, she'll find success.
To the giant called 'Not Good Enough,'
With Me, she'll do her best.
To the giant called 'Fear of Change,'
For comfort, to Me, she'll run."
My Jesus calls out giants
And slays them one by one
In Jesus I find peace and comfort
I find strength for each new day
For I have a blessed assurance
That the giants He will slay.

Going Home

Home is where the heart is
You hear the old folks say
If home is where the heart is,
Then Home's where I want to stay

My home is not on this green earth
Or in the sky aloft
My home is where my Savior lives
And where my mind has wandered oft

In Heaven, one day, I'll stand
But until that blessed day
Upon this earth, I'll trod
For God wishes me to stay

When my job on earth is done
And I write my last great song,
I'll walk into Heaven's gates
And hear my Savior say, "Welcome Home."

Overwhelmed

The darkness surrounds me
I can't see the light
My faith is wavering
I'm overwhelmed by unyielding night

My strength is gone
My faith is weary
My options have run out
My outlook's dreary

I can't see past tomorrow
Or put my hope in today
I'm overwhelmed by the uncontrollable
My faith has gone astray

Alone at the cross
I look up in shame
Overwhelmed by the love
And the life that He gave

His overwhelming grace
Now floods my soul
His overwhelming mercy
My heart now knows

Gentle Shepherd

The Lord is my Shepherd
I've heard many times
With gentle hands He leads me
Through the waters deep and wide

The Lord is my Shepherd
The words echo in my heart
The promise of Scripture
The promise of God

A promise for guidance
A promise of peace
A promise of provision
For a soul filled with grief

The Lord is my Shepherd
Of what shall I fear
Not darkness, not shadow
Not the loss of someone dear

Gentle Shepherd now guide me
Through this valley dark
And help me remember
You're love won't depart

Though shadows surround me
And light I cannot see
The Lord is my Shepherd
Through life, He'll guide me

Perfect Strength

Overwhelmed by life
Waves crashing 'round
Inside the storm rages
Yet I hear this quiet sound

Lost in helplessness
My faith wavers -- then fades
In the darkness
I hear a voice that quietly says:

"Come rest in Me
Come find your peace.
Abide in Me--
Find release.

My strength is perfect
To calm the waves
My strength is perfect
For Me, darkness flees."

A perfect strength I've found
In my Savior divine
Rest for a weary soul
And blessed peace is mine.

Through the Storms

The winds start howling
The rain begins to fall
The water is rising
It's the beginning of a squall

The lightning strikes
The thunder rolls
The temperature drops
It's getting very cold

My body is tired
My soul is weary
The storm rages
The outlook is dreary

In the silence between the thunder
I hear a gentle word
Telling me to be very peaceful
For control is with the Lord

As the storm around me rages
I feel a blessed peace
As quietness floods my soul
And my spirit is at rest

The Lord has seen me through this storm
He'll see me through the rest
I'll rest in His loving arms
Where His comfort is the best

Into His Arms

Come to Me, I hear Him say
Run to Me in the midst of the rain
I'll heal your hurts
I'll heal your pain

You're tired and weary
You can't hold on
You've lost your way
You've lost your song

Come to Me and find your strength
Run to Me and find your rest
Your life, I've planned
I know what's best

I come to Him through the mud and muck
I run to Him through healing rain
I come to Him for comfort and peace
I run into His loving arms again

Nothing But The Blood

Sin stained and broken
I've been washed by the blood
Dark was my heart
I've been washed by the blood

Lost and wondering
I've been washed by the blood
Now found and following
I've been washed by the blood

Washed by the blood
That freely flows
Washed by the blood
That covers my woes

Washed by the blood
Now freely living
Washed by the blood--
The Good News I am giving

The blood of Jesus flows
Urging all to come
For healing and cleansing
To be washed by the blood

Consume Me

Blazing fire of life
Consume the death within
Blazing fire of truth
Consume my life of sin

Blazing fire of hope
Consume all of my doubt
Blazing fire of faith
Consume me from inside out

Consume my heart
Consume my soul
Consume my mind
Consume my whole

My whole life -- consume me
My whole self -- consume me
My whole mind -- consume me
Consume me with You, Lord.

A Christmas Hymn

Infant Child so meek and low
Infant Child in the stable born
Infant Child born that special night
Infant Child sent to be a Light

Holy Child -- to a family born
Holy Child -- in a manger lay
Holy Child -- among mankind lived
Holy Child -- for man would die

Blessed Child Who lived to die
Blessed Child -- the cross He sees
Blessed Child with a call in life
Blessed Child sent to Earth for me

Jesus Christ -- the world can see --
An Infant Child born in humility
This Holy Child lived a sinless life
This Blessed Child -- for me, He died!

Christmas with Jesus

Don't weep for me
I am in a better place
For this Christmas, you see
I can see my Savior's face

The reason you celebrate
This Christmas holiday
Is magnified up here
Where His glory always stays

My dear grieving friend,
Rejoice and cheer
For I am spending Christmas
With Jesus this year

I know that it's hard
To hope and to believe
When memories of Christmases past
Cause your heart to grieve

This Christmas when it's hard
And you feel all alone
Remember I'm with Jesus
And in your heart sing a song

Your song will be merry
And your step will be light
When you remember with Jesus
I'm celebrating tonight.

Ordinary

Ordinary people
In a ordinary world
Called by God
To do ordinary things
Some were fishermen
Some collected taxes
All were ordinary
Nothing special about them

Two thousand years later
Nothing has changed

We are ordinary people
In an ordinary world
Called by God
To do ordinary things
Some are businessmen
Some are parents
All are ordinary
Nothing special about them

Two thousand years later
And everything has changed
We are ordinary people
In an upside down world
Called by God
To do extraordinary things
Some are missionaries
Some are teachers
All are ordinary
Nothing special about us

We are called by God
To make a difference
Wherever we are
Whatever we do
To shine His light
For all to see
To be a friend
To those in need
We are ordinary people
In an upside down world
Called by God
To do extraordinary things

Some are mommies
Some are preachers
All are ordinary
Nothing special about us
To love unconditionally
Those we're called to love
To give sacrificially
To those who are in need
To be a friend to the friendless
A guide to the lost
To be hope to the hopeless
And love everyone at all costs
We are ordinary people
In an upside down world
Called by God
To do extraordinary things
Some are engineers
Some are helpers
All are ordinary
Nothing special about us

Amazed by Grace

Who am I, so sinful and weak,
That I should have audience with God Most High?
Who am I, so hopeless and dead,
That God Almighty would hear me when I cry?
Who am I, so broken and tired,
That Christ, for me, to the cross would go?
Who am I, so unlovely and hurt,
That to me, by Calvary, God's love He did show?
Who am I, so reserved and quiet,
That God calls me to share His love?
Who am I, so earthly and selfish,
That God would prepare me for my Home above?

Loved unconditionally
By God so faithful
For my salvation and grace
Am I eternally grateful
Amazed by this love
Eternally forgiven from sin
Jesus living in my heart
Provides my strength from within
God loves me so much
He accepts me as I live
Jesus died for me
And my sins He forgives
Thank You, Jesus,
For Your eternal love.
Thank You, Jesus,
For my Home above.

The lighthouse has been a very significant symbol for me since my salvation almost 11 years ago. I now remind myself in the midst of a storm that there is a Lighthouse guiding me to safety every day of my life. His name is Jesus and all I have to do is rest in the knowledge that He will never let me drown no matter how hard the storms of life come up against me. God has always given me the hope and strength I need to get through each day no matter how tough it may seem. I pray that others will know this same sense of peace and assurance.

Lighthouse

The storm rises up
So suddenly and strong
The waves crash around
And we wonder how long...

How long will the waves
Crash over me today?
Will I make it through the storm?
Will I make it through the day?

How long will I struggle
Against this storm within?
How long will I struggle
In my habit of sin?

Water fills my boat
And I begin to drown
The weight of my sin
Still pulling me down

Down to the depths
Of sin and despair
Down to the depths
And leaves me there

Gasping for air
Struggling for life
Fighting to swim
Against all this strife

I see above the waves
A Magnificent Light
Calling to me
Relieving my fright
This Light means salvation
This Light equals grace
This light comes from Jesus

And assures me I am safe

The Lighthouse stands tall
Giving me hope
Throwing me a lifeline
To keep me afloat

Jesus is the Lighthouse
Leading all to Him
Freeing all who accept
From the raging storm of sin.

Between The Silence

Endless words
Echo off canyon walls
Wondering if
He hears my calls

Pleas for forgiveness
Prayers for healing
Requests for peace
All His for the giving

Endless words
From my heart to His
Pulling His heartstrings
He hears my calls

Forgiveness for my sins
Healing for my heart
Peace is mine
All His for the giving

Matthew 26:6-13 (NLT)
Meanwhile, Jesus was in Bethany at the home of Simon, a man who had previously had leprosy. While he was eating, a woman came in with a beautiful alabaster jar of expensive perfume and poured it over his head. The disciples were indignant when they saw this. "What a waste!" they said. "It could have been sold for a high price and the money given to the poor." But Jesus, aware of this, replied, "Why criticize this woman for doing such a good thing to me? You will always have the poor among you, but you will not always have me. She has poured this perfume on me to prepare my body for burial. I tell you the truth, wherever the Good News is preached throughout the world, this woman's deed will be remembered and discussed."

My Broken Jar

The worship comes and goes
Because I am only human
My inconsistent life
I pour out before Him
I see the cross
Blood flowing down
Filling to overflowing
My broken jar
The cracks are obvious
The holes are necessary
For You to pour my life
Into those You've given to me
Fill me to overflowing
With Your love divine
So Your life and love
Flow from this broken jar
My broken jar
Poured out for You
Use it for Your glory
Use me - I'm Yours.

Anger Resolution
(A Prayer)

The anger explodes inside
Rage I cannot control
Against an enemy I cannot see
Against those whose hand I've held

The anger rages within
From a source I cannot see
Against an enemy whose voice I hear
Against bondage -- longing to be free

I long for freedom from anger
I long for peace and calm
I long for Your mercy
And Your healing balm

To the cross I come
I lay my burden down
At Your bloody feet
My anger -- now Your crown

Help me find a freedom
From all my anger and pain
Help me live in freedom
Experiencing forgiveness all my days

Through the Fire

You see my struggle
You know my pain
You hear the voices
You feel my shame

You see my tears
You know my thoughts
You hear my confession
You feel my beating heart

I want Your oil of healing
To wash right over me
I want Your peace everlasting
To fill the void within me

Fill my longing heart
With Your love divine
Hold my wavering hand
And lead me by Your side

Through waters deep
You hold my hand
Through fires hot
With me, You stand

Overwhelmed by my circumstances
I come to the cross divine
Washed by Your precious blood
I find blessed peace is mine

Clouds are always white from the sky-view, even if they are dark and gloomy from the ground.

Above The Clouds

From where I stand,
Dark clouds hover around
There's a storm on the horizon--
Deep, dark, black clouds
The rain begins to fall
The thunder starts to roll
The lightening strikes around
The storm is taking its toll
From where I stand,
Wet and afraid
I hear Your calm voice
And this is what You say:

"From above the clouds,
The sky is bright.
From above the clouds,
You are in My sight
I see the storm
I see your fear
Just know, My child,
That I am here
I'll hold you close
I'll never stray
By your side
Through every day
Though storms may come
And fear abounds
Just know, My child,
I'm above the clouds."

From where I stand
The sky is dark
The road is long
The day is hard
The potholes are many
The curves are sharp
I've lost my way
Not sure where to start.
From where I stand
Bruised and battered
I hear Your calm voice

And this is what You say:

"From above the clouds,
The road is straight.
From above the clouds,
I'll keep you safe
I see the road
I see your fear
Just know, My child,
That I am here
I'll hold you close
I'll never stray
By your side
Through every day
Though roads aren't straight
And rocks abound
Just know, My child,
I'm above the clouds."

I Am His

Beaten down
Defeated
Broken
Knocked over
Toyed with
Hurt

The pain is real
The torment never ends
Hearing all my failures
Reliving all my sins
This voice keeps nagging
Telling me I'm alone
Telling me I'm not loved
Telling me it's my fault

But then, I hear a voice
A quiet whisper
Telling me I am His
And then, I feel tender hands
Gently wrapping
Holding me -- I am His

I am His child
Loved by the Eternal God
Nothing can change this
No matter what anyone says
He upholds me
Forever with His hands
Keeps me from falling
Out of His grasp

Held

You formed the world
With only one command
But yet You hold me
In the palm of Your hand

You made the universe--
The grandeur of space
But still in Your hand
My heart has found a place

The storms You allow
May knock me down
But always in Your hand
Peace and safety may be found

So gently You hold me
Though winds may wail
I'll stay in Your hand
'Cause your grip will not fail

So tenderly You'll hold me
Until at last I will see
Your face in Heaven--
The One Who held me

A Thanksgiving Psalm

For creating me
And giving me life,
To God, I am grateful.
For guiding me
And loving their child,
To my parents, I am grateful.
For carrying me
Through life's tough trials,
To Jesus, I am grateful.
For loving me
Through those cold, dark nights,
To my Love, I am grateful.
For leading me
In the choices that are right
Holy Spirit, I am grateful.

I am grateful to be spared
From the trials many face
I am grateful to be carried
By God's amazing grace

I am grateful to be loved
By so many around the Earth
I am grateful that I learned
In my life, put Jesus first

Take my grateful heart
An offering I bring
To share the love of God
For all this Thanksgiving

Still Night

In an humble manger
On a peaceful hill
A Baby's cry
Breaks the night's still
On the quiet countryside
In a peaceful field
A host of angels
Breaks the night's still
In a country far east
Wise astrologers lived
A star was seen
That breaks the night's still
Child of God
In human form
On this still night
To us is born

This Child -- He grew
As God and Man
To live on Earth--
Salvation's Plan
On a Hill called Calvary
Under a veil of night
"It is finished!"
Breaks the still of the night
In a cold, dark heart
Overcome by fright
Life was changed
Because of a Baby's cry

Do not fear, for I am with you; do not be afraid, for I am your God. I will hold on to you with My righteous right hand. Isaiah 40:11

Promises For The New Year

As the old year comes to an end
And I look back at the places I've been
I find places of sorrow and places of joy
I find places of unrest and places of peace

As the old year comes to an end
And a new journey begins,
His peace floods my heart
His Spirit quiets mine

I hear Him whisper, "Peace, My child
Your life, I hold
I'll walk with you
Through what seems unknown

Your life, I'll guide
Through the darkest time.
When life seems unsure,
Place your hand in Mine."

My Valentine

Preschool love --
Will you hold my hand?
I love my teacher.
Let's go play in the sand
Will you be my Valentine?

First grade comes
And friendships grow
Cards are passed --
Parties thrown
Will you be my Valentine?

Third grade now
Notes in class
Do you love me
Is the question asked
Will you be my Valentine?

Middle school
Brings awkward times
Holding hands
In the lunchroom line
Will you be my Valentine?

High school prom
What a special time
Dancing close
With your hands in mine
Will you be my Valentine?

Years go by and love grows
A ring in his hand
On one bent knee
Her hand in his hand
Will you be my Valentine?

Perfect love on a wooden cross
Living love
Living proof
Shed His blood
Will you be my Valentine?

A Thanksgiving Psalm

For creating me
And giving me life,
To God, I am grateful.

For guiding me
And loving their child,
To my parents, I am grateful.

For carrying me
Through life's tough trials,
To Jesus, I am grateful.

For loving me
Through those cold, dark nights,
To my Love, I am grateful.

For leading me
In the choices that are right
Holy Spirit, I am grateful.

I am grateful to be spared
From the trials many face
I am grateful to be carried
By God's amazing grace

I am grateful to be loved
By so many around the Earth
I am grateful that I learned
In my life, put Jesus first

Take my grateful heart
An offering I bring
To share the love of God
For all this Thanksgiving

Above The Clouds

From where I stand,
Dark clouds hover around
There's a storm on the horizon--
Deep, dark, black clouds

The rain begins to fall
The thunder starts to roll
The lightening strikes around
The storm is taking its toll

From where I stand,
Wet and afraid
I hear Your calm voice
And this is what You say:

"From above the clouds,
The sky is bright.
From above the clouds,
You are in My sight

I see the storm
I see your fear
Just know, My child,
That I am here

I'll hold you close
I'll never stray
By your side
Through every day

Though storms may come
And fear abounds
Just know, My child,
I'm above the clouds."

From where I stand
The sky is dark
The road is long
The day is hard

The potholes are many
The curves are sharp
I've lost my way
Not sure where to start.

From where I stand
Bruised and battered
I hear Your calm voice
And this is what You say:

"From above the clouds,
The road is straight.
From above the clouds,
I'll keep you safe

I see the road
I see your fear
Just know, My child,
That I am here

I'll hold you close
I'll never stray
By your side
Through every day

Though roads aren't straight
And rocks abound
Just know, My child,
I'm above the clouds."

Amazed by Grace

Who am I, so sinful and weak,
That I should have audience with God Most High?
Who am I, so hopeless and dead,
That God Almighty would hear me when I cry?

Who am I, so broken and tired,
That Christ, for me, to the cross would go?
Who am I, so unlovely and hurt,
That to me, by Calvary, God's love He did show?

Who am I, so reserved and quiet,
That God calls me to share His love?
Who am I, so earthly and selfish,
That God would prepare me for my Home above?

Loved unconditionally
By God so faithful
For my salvation and grace
Am I eternally grateful

Amazed by this love
Eternally forgiven from sin
Jesus living in my heart
Provides my strength from within

God loves me so much
He accepts me as I live
Jesus died for me
And my sins He forgives

Thank You, Jesus,
For Your eternal love.
Thank You, Jesus,
For my Home above.

In Your Presence

In Your presence, the darkness flees
In Your presence, our fears are stilled
In Your presence, the devil trembles
In Your presence, our hearts are filled

In Your presence, our souls are quieted
In Your presence, demons fall
In Your presence, our hands are lifted
In Your presence, we give our all

In Your presence, there is healing
In Your presence, there is grace
In Your presence, there is hope
In Your presence, we stand amazed

In Your presence, You bring freedom
In Your presence, You bring peace
In Your presence, we lift our eyes
In Your presence, our hearts are at ease

My Broken Jar

The worship comes and goes
Because I am only human
My inconsistent life
I pour out before Him

I see the cross
Blood flowing down
Filling to overflowing
My broken jar

The cracks are obvious
The holes are necessary
For You to pour my life
Into those You've given to me

Fill me to overflowing
With Your love divine
So Your life and love
Flow from this broken jar

My broken jar
Poured out for You
Use it for Your glory
Use me - I'm Yours.

Between The Silence

Endless words
Echo off canyon walls
Wondering if
He hears my calls

Pleas for forgiveness
Prayers for healing
Requests for peace
All His for the giving

Endless words
From my heart to His
Pulling His heartstrings
He hears my calls

Forgiveness for my sins
Healing for my heart
Peace is mine
All His for the giving

Ordinary

Ordinary people
In a ordinary world
Called by God
To do ordinary things
Some were fishermen
Some collected taxes
All were ordinary
Nothing special about them

Two thousand years later
Nothing has changed

We are ordinary people
In an ordinary world
Called by God
To do ordinary things
Some are businessmen
Some are parents
All are ordinary
Nothing special about them

Two thousand years later
And everything has changed

We are ordinary people
In an upside down world
Called by God
To do extraordinary things
Some are missionaries
Some are teachers
All are ordinary
Nothing special about us

We are called by God
To make a difference
Wherever we are
Whatever we do
To shine His light
For all to see
To be a friend
To those in need

We are ordinary people
In an upside down world

Called by God
To do extraordinary things
Some are mommies
Some are preachers
All are ordinary
Nothing special about us

To love unconditionally
Those we're called to love
To give sacrificially
To those who are in need
To be a friend to the friendless
A guide to the lost
To be hope to the hopeless
And love everyone at all costs

We are ordinary people
In an upside down world
Called by God
To do extraordinary things
Some are engineers
Some are helpers
All are ordinary
Nothing special about us

A Christmas Hymn

Infant Child so meek and low
Infant Child in the stable born
Infant Child born that special night
Infant Child sent to be a Light

Holy Child -- to a family born
Holy Child -- in a manger lay
Holy Child -- among mankind lived
Holy Child -- for man would die

Blessed Child Who lived to die
Blessed Child -- the cross He sees
Blessed Child with a call in life
Blessed Child sent to Earth for me

Jesus Christ -- the world can see --
An Infant Child born in humility
This Holy Child lived a sinless life
This Blessed Child -- for me, He died!

A Christmas Gift

Looking into the face of a baby
She really had no clue
What the Infant in her arms
Would grow up to do

She knew the Child was special—
She knew He was divine
She did not know that He'd grow up
To change the water into wine

She knew she was holding royalty
She knew it was the face of a King
But she did not know that her baby
Would be no earthly King

She did not know God's ultimate plan
She only knew her part
From this Infant Child within her arms
God's redemption plan would start

She did not know the pain she'd face
When Christ was nailed to a tree
But she did know the truth
That He died for you and me.

Christmas Memories

Gathered 'round the fire
Singing Christmas songs
With Mom at the piano
Oh has it been so long?

Silent nights and little towns
Jingle Bells and Deck the Halls
The First Noel and Three Wise Men
The words - I know them all

And as each Christmas draweth close
Those age-old songs I hear
Reminding me all the time
That at Christmas you aren't here

The tears - they overwhelm me
I cannot make them end
'Cause when you died
I lost in you a very special friend

Written in honor of and memory of my Dado Christmas 2006

0If Mary Had Said No

If Mary had said no,
Would God have still sent His Son?
If Mary had said no,
Would Jesus have come to save everyone?

If Mary had said no,
Would there be no hope for the world?
If Mary had said no,
Would there be more people out in the cold?

If Mary had said no,
Would the disciples have had Someone to follow?
If Mary had said no,
Would the Pharisees have Someone to put down?

If Mary had said no,
Would God's love have been demonstrated?
If Mary had said no,
Would Jesus' blood have been shed?

But Mary said yes,
And much to our delight,
Brought into this world
A brilliant and glorious Light

A Christmas Gift

Looking into the face of a baby
She really had no clue
What the Infant in her arms
Would grow up to do

She knew the Child was special—
She knew He was divine
She did not know that He'd grow up
To change the water into wine

She knew she was holding royalty
She knew it was the face of a King
But she did not know that her baby
Would be no earthly King

She did not know God's ultimate plan
She only knew her part
From this Infant Child within her arms
God's redemption plan would start

She did not know the pain she'd face
When Christ was nailed to a tree
But she did know the truth
That He died for you and me.

Christmas with Jesus

Don't weep for me
I am in a better place
For this Christmas, you see
I can see my Savior's face

The reason you celebrate
This Christmas holiday
Is magnified up here
Where His glory always stays

My dear grieving friend,
Rejoice and cheer
For I am spending Christmas
With Jesus this year

I know that it's hard
To hope and to believe
When memories of Christmases past
Cause your heart to grieve

This Christmas when it's hard
And you feel all alone
Remember I'm with Jesus
And in your heart sing a song

Your song will be merry
And your step will be light
When you remember with Jesus
I'm celebrating tonight.

Grace

Broken, Battered, Worn, and Spent
I enter Your Holy Place
Tired, Frustrated, Beaten Down
To see Your Cross of Grace

Angry, Hurting, Confused, and Afraid
I enter Your Holy Place
Distressed, Weary, as Sinful Man
I come to Your Throne of Grace

Forgiven, Revived, Hopeful, and Blessed
I enter Your Holy Place
Covered by Your Blood, Redeemed and Free
I come to the Table of Grace

To partake in Your Forgiveness
To renew my wavering faith
To receive Grace for the Day
I feast from the Table of Grace

Loved and Healed, Free and Empowered
No longer broken, I seek Your Holy Face
I find eternal peace and safety
On my knees before the Throne of Grace

Simple Trust

Tis so sweet to trust in Jesus
The great old hymn rings out
Trusting Jesus every day
Faith and hope - no room for doubt

O how sweet to trust in Jesus
Daily trusting through it all
Holding to the Cross
No matter what befalls

Yes! Tis sweet to trust in Jesus!
My heart will ever sing
Though doubt may filter in
Remind me, Jesus, to trust in everything

I'm so glad I've learned to trust Him
Jesus leads me in the way
No matter what struggles come
I'll simply trust Him every day

Dancing in the Streets of Heaven

No more aches
No more pain
Dancing in the streets of Heaven
No more sorrow
No more shame
Dancing on the streets of Heaven

No more loneliness
Seeing loved ones again
Dancing on the streets of Heaven
No mores sickness
Alive again
Dancing on the streets of Heaven

Now she sees Him
Faith to face
Dancing on the streets of Heaven
Worship forever
At the Throne of Grace
Dancing on the streets of Heaven

Family and friends,
See your loved ones now
Dancing on the streets of Heaven
No more pain
His Love abounds
Dancing in the streets of Heaven

In Memory of Grandma Bobbie (Barbara Bradley)

Because

Because of a man,
Sin entered the world
A mistake was made
The heart was made cold

Because of their sin,
God sent a great rain
To wash everything away
To start fresh again

Because of a man,
God created a nation --
A people of His own
A beautiful creation

Because of a man
Who became a great king
A heritage was started
To reunite God with man again

Because of a Baby
Born in a stable with sheep
God became flesh
And with man He would keep

That Baby grew up,
Becoming a Man
Teaching the masses
About the Master's Plan

Because of love
That Man died on a cross
Because of compassion
To save all who were lost

Because of salvation
My heart sings today
Because of His grace
I live in love each day

Because of the Garden
Because of the Manger
Because of the Cross

I don't face His anger

Because of the heritage I was given
Jesus lives in my heart today
Because of the cross
I am free to say:

Jesus loves me --
This I know
Jesus loves me
The Cross -- it shows

It shows a Love
That was there in the Garden
It shows a Promise
For the Here and the After

Out of Darkness

It's not real, they say, --
This pain that you feel.
The wounds he inflicted
Have had time to heal

The scars, they say,--
Only make us stronger
As I patiently wait,
Tell me how much longer

How much long till the rescue?
How much longer till I'm free?
How much longer must I run
From a past that torments me?

How much longer must I carry
This heavy burden alone?
How much longer must I wait
For the past to make me strong?

From out of the darkness
Speaking through the pain
I hear a still, strong voice
Just trust Me again.

Trust Me with your darkness
Trust Me with your pain
Trust that I am working
To make you strong again

The Love of Jesus

Jesus loves me, this I know
A preschool song learned long ago
With a catchy tune and words well known,
To soothe a child, you sing the song.

Jesus loves me, this I know
This song we teach as we watch them grow
From inocent lips we hear them sing
This proclamation of love from Jesus the King

Jesus loves me, we hear them say
When they give their hearts to Jesus one day
With joy in their hearts and a song in their soul
Singing Jesus loves me, this I know.

The love of Jesus so great and vast
Will shine to the world till the very last
When children sing with all their soul
Jesus loves me, this I know.

Simple Trust

Tis so sweet to trust in Jesus
The great old hymn rings out
Trusting Jesus every day
Faith and hope -- no room for doubt

O how sweet to trust in Jesus
Daily trusting through it all
Holding closely to the cross
No matter what ever befalls

Yes! Tis sweet to trust in Jesus!
My heart will ever sing
Though doubt and fear may filter in
Remind me, Jesus, to trust in everything

I'm so glad I've learned to trust Him
Jesus leads me all the way
No matter what struggles come
I'll simply trust Him every day

Because

Because of a man,
Sin entered the world
A mistake was made
The heart was made cold

Because of their sin,
God sent a great rain
To wash everything away
To start fresh again

Because of a man,
God created a nation --
A people of His own
A beautiful creation

Because of a man
Who became a great king
A heritage was started
To reunite God with man again

Because of a Baby
Born in a stable with sheep
God became flesh
And with man He would keep

That Baby grew up,
Becoming a Man
Teaching the masses
About the Master's Plan

Because of love
That Man died on a cross
Because of compassion
To save all who were lost

Because of salvation
My heart sings today
Because of His grace
I live in love each day

Because of the Garden
Because of the Manger
Because of the Cross
I don't face His anger

Because of the heritage I was given
Jesus lives in my heart today
Because of the cross
I am free to say:

Jesus loves me --
This I know
Jesus loves me
The Cross -- it shows

It shows a Love
That was there in the Garden
It shows a Promise
For the Here and the After

Given

A name she was given
For a time not yet come
A promise from the Lord
For a child not yet born

Patiently she tries to wait
For God's perfect time displayed
When sleeping in her arms
Is this child for whom she prays

She does not know the why
Or even when or how
She wants to trust her Savior
Until He shows her "now"

With broken heart she prays
With every month she waits
Longing in her heart
For this child for whom she prays

She cries out in her praying
"Oh, God, why can't there be
A baby in my arms
Snuggled up to me?

Oh, God, this child You promised -
His name is in Your Word
It's meaning You have shown me -
"I have asked of the Lord"

Sweet Samuel is chosen
For an appointed time and place
So Father, in my impatience,
Impart on me Your grace

I need Your grace to fill me
Around those who are with child
And help me not be bitter
Lord, help me to be mild

Help me love these children
Without bitterness or disgust
While waiting oh so long

And learning in You to trust

Week of Hope

Sunday, crowds shout "Hosanna"
As He walks in down through the street
They line up with palm branches waiving
Waiting for the King to meet

Monday, disciples still follow Him
Not believing what He said
In a few short days, their song will change -
They will want this Prophet dead

Tuesday, many still follow
Needing miracles performed
Not remembering the Scriptures
In which His end is warned

Wednesday's bread is broken
As He goes to the Garden to pray
Knowing that very soon
Judas - chosen - will betray

Thursday is filled with trials
And accusations rang out loud
Then Pilate washed his hands
And gave Jesus to the crowd

Friday's filled with flogging
And nails on a rugged cross
The world now filled with darkness
As He hung there for souls lost

Saturday was silent
As He lay there in the grave
Their hopes and dreams were shattered
They will never be the same

In the darkness on that Sunday,
The stone was rolled away
To show the world that Jesus lives
And He's alive in us today

Darkness Dies

In the beginning there was darkness
Hovering over the face of the deep
Awaiting the Spirit of God
Whose voice was about to speak

Let there be light
And the darkness was gone
In six short days,
Creation sang its song

Soon there was darkness
In the form of sin
That covers our souls
And kills from within

This cannot happen
Roared the Lion of Grace
The world turned away
Refusing to see His face

God sent His Light
From our sins to save us
This Light shines to all
His name is Jesus

This Man named Jesus
Lived a sinless life
Teaching those around Him
To live in peace, not in strife

No Longer A Slave

Once bound in darkness
Enshrouded by sin
Wandering alone
With no light at the end

Once held captive
By chains from the past
Dreaming of freedom
And peace that will last

A slave to death
A slave to sin
Bound by heavy chains
Hidden deep within

To the Cross running
Encumbered by chains
Falling at His feet
Searching for freedom again

No longer a slave
Bound by shame and sin
Freedom is going
When Christ is within

The Cross brings freedom
Too those He has saved
The chains of sin -- broken --
No long enslaved

No longer a slave
To the sins of this life
Now freely enslaved
As a Child of Christ

Hope Alive in Me

Perfect creation
Made for Your glory
Living creatures
To tell Your story

Perfect man
In a perfect world
Tempted by Satan
Forgetting God's word

Perfect lives
Now stained with sin
Perfect relationship
Broken again

Perfect plan
Began that day
God's perfect Lamb
To take sins away

Hope began
With a promise of life
Sacrifice for sin
And freedom from strife

Hope revealed
In a Baby's face
Born in a stable
The Person of grace

Hope walked the earth
With sinful man
Teaching the Kingdom
How to be born again

Hope put on trial
For our crime He did pay
Hope remained silent
Bore our sin and shame

Hope nailed to the Cross
Darkness over the land
Hope breathed His last

God's grace revealed with His mighty hand

Hope placed in the grave
It seemed all Hope was lost
Cries from the crowds
Christ died at a cost

Early the third day
The stone was rolled away
Hope alive again
And Hope still lives today

Hope lives in our hearts
Hope gives us grace
Hope alive in us
Providing perfect peace

Hope coming back one day
His children to gather
And we'll live in Heaven
Eternity with the Father

Week of Hope

Sunday, crowds shout "Hosanna"
As He walks in down through the street
They line up with palm branches waiving
Waiting for the King to meet

Monday, disciples still follow Him
Not believing what He said
In a few short days, their song will change -
They will want this Prophet dead

Tuesday, many still follow
Needing miracles performed
Not remembering the Scriptures
In which His end is warned

Wednesday's bread is broken
As He goes to the Garden to pray
Knowing that very soon
Judas - chosen - will betray

Thursday is filled with trials
And accusations rang out loud
Then Pilate washed his hands
And gave Jesus to the crowd

Friday's filled with flogging
And nails on a rugged cross
The world now filled with darkness
As He hung there for souls lost

Saturday was silent
As He lay there in the grave
Their hopes and dreams were shattered
They will never be the same

In the darkness on that Sunday,
The stone was rolled away
To show the world that Jesus lives
And He's alive in us today

For as many as are the promises of God, in Christ they are [all answered] "Yes." So through Him we say our "Amen" to the glory of God. 2 CORINTHIANS 1:20 AMP

For every one of God's promises is "Yes" in Him. Therefore, the "Amen" is also spoken through Him by us for God's glory. 2 Corinthians 1:20 HCSB

Hannah's Cry

I know I heard Your voice
Spoken loud and clear
The promise that You've given
Spoken gently in my ear

"Your desire for a child
Has been heard from afar
Your cries have reached Heaven
And touched the Father's heart.

One sweet day I'll deliver
This child into your arms
A child for you to love
And and protect from worldly harm

Until the day you meet this child
Wait patiently on Me
And love the ones I've given you
About My love to teach

My promises are Yes
And in My Son Amen
I hear your silent cries
Your prayers have reached Heaven

The heart of God is moved
When His people pray
He hears our every prayer
And answers then with grace

He promises every answer
Will come in His perfect time
If we pray in faith
And in His Word abide

Broken Pieces

It's hard
They're deep
The scars within my soul

The pain
It's real
I long to be made whole

My soul
Was crushed
When you left without a word

My life
In shambles
My spirit weak - and worn

My heart
It's hard
The grudge still runs deep

The Cross
It says
Forgiveness is the key

Let go
Forgive
The hurt you hold down deep

A crown
He holds
Reminds me I am His

His grace
He gifts
I am free to forgive

Finding Solace in the Saviour

Quietly He calls
From a world filled with strife
Peacefully He walks
Beside us through this short life

Gently He guides
Down the narrow path
Lovingly He frees us
From His condemning wrath

Arrogantly we sit
Waiting for God to speak
Impatiently we pace
Even when our faith is weak

Angrily we cry
Wanting Him to move
Stubbornly we run
Away from forgiving love

Break us, oh Lord,
Make our hearts broken
Over our sins
Over the Word You've spoken

Bring us to repentance
Bring us to grace
As we seek Your perfect will
As we seek Your holy Face

Forgive us, oh Lord,
Bring us from our wayward path
Wash us clean, oh Lord,
From the sins both present and past

Forgive us, oh Lord,
Fill us with Your grace
Heal us, oh Lord,
As we bow in Your Holy Place

We bow before the Cross
Repentant and broken
Search us, oh Lord,
We confess to be forgiven

We bow before the Cross
Forgiven and humble
Daily asking forgiveness
For each and every stumble

Into the world, we are called
To show a world Your grace
To share with them forgiveness
And teach them to seek Your face

Into the world, we are called
To make disciples of all men
To share with them the peace
That You have placed within

The Love of Jesus

Jesus loves me, this I know
A preschool song learned long ago
With a catchy tune and words well known
To soothe a child, you sing the song

Jesus loves me, this I know
This song we teach as we watch them grow
From innocent lips we hear them sing
This proclamation of love from Jesus, the King

Jesus loves me, we hear them say
When they give their hearts to Jesus one day
With joy in their hearts and a song in their soul
Singing Jesus loves me, this I know

The love of Jesus, so great and vast
Will shine to the world till the very last
When children sing with all their soul
Jesus loves me, this I know

Out of Darkness

It's not real, they say, --
This pain that you feel.
The wounds he inflicted
Have had time to heal

The scars, they say,--
Only make us stronger
As I patiently wait,
Tell me how much longer

How much long till the rescue?
How much longer till I'm free?
How much longer must I run
From a past that torments me?

How much longer must I carry
This heavy burden alone?
How much longer must I wait
For the past to make me strong?

From out of the darkness
Speaking through the pain
I hear a still, strong voice
Just trust Me again.

Trust Me with your darkness
Trust Me with your pain
Trust that I am working
To make you strong again

When you are at your weakest
And every day is hard,
Trust I have a plan
Trust that I am God

Simple Trust

Tis so sweet to trust in Jesus
The great old hymn rings out
Trusting Jesus every day
Faith and hope - no room for doubt

O how sweet to trust in Jesus
Daily trusting through it all
Holding to the Cross
No matter what befalls

Yes! Tis sweet to trust in Jesus!
My heart will ever sing
Though doubt may filter in
Remind me, Jesus, to trust in everything

I'm so glad I've learned to trust Him
Jesus leads me in the way
No matter what struggles come
I'll simply trust Him every day

Throne of Grace

Broken, Battered, Worn, and Spent
I enter Your Holy Place
Tired, Frustrated, Beaten Down
To see Your Cross of Grace

Angry, Hurting, Confused, and Afraid
I enter Your Holy Place
Distressed, Weary, as Sinful Man
I come to Your Throne of Grace

Forgiven, Revived, Hopeful, and Blessed
I enter Your Holy Place
Covered by Your Blood, Redeemed and Free
I come to the Table of Grace

To partake in Your Forgiveness
To renew my wavering faith
To receive Grace for the Day
I feast from the Table of Grace

Loved and Healed, Free and Empowered
No longer broken, I seek Your Holy Face
I find eternal peace and safety
On my knees before the Throne of Grace

Jesus Came Down

Abandoned by disciples
Beaten by bystanders
Crucified by crowds
Displayed between thieves
Friday seemed dark and desolate

Laid in a borrowed tomb
Wrapped in pieces of cloth
Stone sealed tomb
Soldiers guard the body
Saturday seemed hopeless and empty

Walking in the Garden
Speaking with Mary
Stone rolled away
Soldiers sleeping
Sunday was dawning

Dark and desolate
Hopeless and empty
Longing for hope
Longing for healing
We come searching

Searching on the cross
Searching in the tomb
Walking in the garden
Walking on the road
We search for salvation

In the stillness of the night
In every tear that falls
In the warmth of the sunshine
And every smile that's shared
He lives and brings His peace

To set free every captive
To loosen Satan's grasp
To bring us closer to Heaven
To show us how to live
Jesus came down

Beauty From Ashes

A broken heart
A tattered soul
A desperate cry --
A desire to be whole

A weary spirit
Battered and worn
Bowed at the altar
For a word from the LORD

"A trial by fire
You must endure
To make you clean
And make you pure

I'll take the ashes
Sweep them away
I'll make it beautiful
So in the end you'll say,

'My heart rejoices
My spirit soars
My soul is resting
In Jesus, my LORD.'

He took my ashes
And made them clay
To form me into
Who I am today.

Thank You, Jesus,
For the trial by fire.
Thank You, LORD,
For refining my desire.

To be lead by You
Is my only aim
So that "Well done"
I'll hear one day.

Do not fear, for I am with you; do not be afraid, for I am your God. I will strengthen you; I will help you; I will hold on to you with My righteous right hand. (Isaiah 41:10 HCSB)

Promise For The New Year

As the old year comes to an end
And I look back upon the places I've been,
I find places of sorrow and places of joy
I find places of unrest and places of peace

As the old year comes to an end
And I look back at the people I've met,
I've seen the hurting and hopeful
I've seen the grieving and joyful

As the old year comes to an end
And a new journey begins,
His peace floods my heart
His Spirit quiets mine.

I hear Him whisper "Peace, My child.
Your life, I hold.
I'll walk with you
Through what seems unknown.

Your life, I'll guide
Through the darkest time.
When life seems unsure,
Place your hand in Mine."

You Are

You are the One Who spoke creation
Into existence with Your Voice
You are the One Who placed the tree
In the Garden to give a choice

When Man chose pleasure
Rather than chosing to obey
You are the One Who had a plan-
A purpose, a will, a way

When the world became so wicked
And You wanted to start again
You told a man named Noah
To build an ark to save his kin

All the while, the world spins on
While Prophets speak of a Man
This Man more righteous than Adam
Who will save the world from sin

This man named Jesus -
Born of a humble birth
Came to die on the cross
Because that's what Man is worth

When storms arise and darkness comes
And it seems you've lost your way
Just fold your hands, get on your knees
Cry out to Him and pray:

You are still God. You made the storms.
And though ahead I cannot see
I know that You are still God
And through the dark, You'll carry me.

Searching for Joy

Broken and battered
By lies from the World
Desperately clinging
To a promise from her Lord

Weak and wounded
By family and friends
Wanting her joy back
Looking for peace again

Another Sunday morning
She puts on her Sunday mask
Heads into church quickly
To avoid questions being asked

She walks into the Sanctuary
And quietly takes her seat
Waiting for service to start
Eagerly wanting her Savior meet

The music starts playing
And she listens to the words
Praying so intently
Wanting her prayers to be heard

The songs move her to tears
Reminding her of His faithfulness
But still she often questions
His words and His promises

The sermon speaks to her heart
She listens with expectancy
Craving healing for her soul
Waiting for Him to speak

The invitation is given to all
She stands and silently prays
Exchanging her dreams for His
Pledging surrender for all of her days

Worshipping and waiting
Holding on to a prayer
Holding to the promise

That God is always there

A Quiet Grief: Desiring To Be Called Mommy

It is just another Sunday to her
She quickly takes her seat
She sees families gathered around her
She quietly begins to weep

Everywhere she looks is a trigger
There are children all around
She bows her head in shame and despair
Wanting to sink into the ground

"You're like their second momma"
She hears so many say
But in her heart she is grieving
There's no one to celebrate her today

She yearns for a child to call her own
She longs to hear laughter as children play
Her desire is to be called "Momma"
And have a reason to celebrate this day

Another Mother's Day will come and go
She'll place a smile upon her face
She'll pray earnestly and sincerely
For God to give her grace

She hears Him whisper softly
"My child, I see your grief.
Keep holding to My promises
And I will bring you peace."

Even Now

You created the world
In six short days
Even then, You had a plan

Mankind rebelled
Sin ruled the world
Even then, You had a plan

The earth, You flooded
To rid the world of sin
Even then, You had a plan

Through kings and prophets,
Your people lived
Even then, You had a plan

You watched Your plan unfold
From the beginning of time
Your plan in place

To save the world
From Sin and Shame
Your plan to send Jesus

To live a sinless life
To bear our cross
Jesus' plan to save us

Even then, Your plan
Visible through the ages
Carried out in perfect timing

Even now, I hear You
You've whispered a name
Even now, I know You have a plan

Even now, I'll trust You.
Even when I can't see Your Plan
I'll lay my plan down

Even when the way seems dark
Even when I can't see Your had
I will chose to trust You

Even now, the way seems impossible
Even now, I hear Your voice
Your call bids me peace

Even now, patiently I'll wait
Joyfully waiting and hoping
For the promise You've given

Even now, You're working
Even now, You're good
Even now, You love me

Even now, You give peace
Even now, Your plan unfolds
Even now, You bid me wait

Even if Your promise is delayed
Even if I lose heart
I'll still chose to praise You

Even though I cannot see Your hand
Even though I do not know your plan,
I'll still chose to trust You.

Even when You fulfill Your promise
Even when this heart is healed
I'll praise You forever

CPSIA information can be obtained
at www.ICGtesting.com
Printed in the USA
BVHW080127090919
557876BV00014BA/1616/P